Volume 6
Decodable
Reader

Mc
Graw
Hill
Education

Bothell, WA • Chicago, IL • Columbus, OH • New York, NY

Contents

Herb's Dinner

by Julie Palmer
illustrated by Meryl Henderson

Herb was a hungry turtle. He set
out to find his dinner. He liked to
eat tender, sweet ferns. Ferns
made a perfect dinner.

Herb spotted some ferns. He
wanted to get to them fast. Herb
told himself that perhaps he
could climb the biggest rock first.

Oh no! Herb flopped on his back.
He was not hurt but he was stuck.
He lurched and jerked. He could
not budge. Herb alerted a bird
flying past.

The bird perched on the rock.
It began to chirp. A girl was close by.
She spotted the bird.
Then she spotted Herb on the dirt.

Herb looked like the saddest turtle the girl had ever seen.

"Let me help," said the girl. She turned Herb over. "That's better," she whispered.

Herb was grateful. He returned to getting the ferns. This time he went around the rocks. It didn't matter that it was slower. Herb was not in a hurry.

Howdy, Partner!

by Kim Anderson

illustrated by Karen Tafoya

The car ride to the ranch was far. Carla, Mom, and Dad checked into the cabin. Rancher Mark greeted them.

"Howdy, partners!" he smiled. "Let's go meet the horses."

"This is the smartest horse in these parts," said Rancher Bert. "Her name is White Star."

"She is charming," clapped Carla. "May I ride on White Star?"

Bert helped Carla get on.

"Step in the stirrup," said Bert. "Now lift up your arms. Let's start riding, partner!"

The trail led far and wide. The ranchers led the way. Carla, Mom, and Dad rode behind.

"This is like a postcard," Carla remarked.

Carla and Rancher Marvin posed for Dad.

"Say cheese!" said Dad.

"That's a darling shot," smiled Mom.

Carla squeezed in a roping
lesson before it got dark.
Rancher Marge showed her
how to swing her arm.

"You worked hard today," said Rancher Mark. "Set your alarm. We will start riding after sunrise. You'll need to be sharp."

"I will!" Carla exclaimed.

Chores on a Farm

by Rich Bennett

illustrated by Karen Tafoya

Dora was born on a farm. Each
morning, she gets up before
five a.m. Then Dora sets her
feet on the floor. She has a lot
of chores.

Dad turns on the porch light.

"I bet other children are sleeping," Dora thinks. "I wish I did not have to get up. But at least I get to be with my horse, Glory."

Dora follows Dad. It is still dark.

"I'll wish upon a star," Dora thinks.
"But what can I wish for? I know!
I wish for no more chores!"

Dora brings in water for the cows. Dad brings in corn and grain from the feed store.

"Soon, I will finish," Dora thinks to herself. "Then I will ride Glory."

Dora jumps on her horse. She rides as the night turns to day.

"Faster! Faster, Glory!" Dora yells. Glory races on.

Dora smiles. She strokes Glory. The sun is up!

"I do not like chores," she thinks. "But I do like riding my horse in the morning!"

DEAR JACK

by Imani Brown

illustrated by Betty Leitzman

Is Jack near? Did Jack hear?
Did Jack rip Kim's red kite?

Is Jack near? Did Jack hear?
Did Jack eat Dad's new socks?

Is Jack near? Did Jack hear?
Did Jack bite Brad's backpack?

28

Is Jack near? Did Jack hear?
Did Jack snack on Gran's book?

Is Jack near? Did Jack hear?
Is Jack inside hiding in fear?

Oh, dear!
Jack is not near! Jack is not here!
He is not outside. He is not inside.

Jack, come here!
You have nothing to fear!

31

Jack's bark was so sincere.

Kim smiled and pet him, "Oh, Jack!
Oh, dear!"

Not There!

by Kevin Harmon

illustrated by Mary Kurnick Maass

"Dad, can we fly my chopper in Bear Park later?" Martin asked.

"I told Claire we would go to the museum," Dad shared.

Dad and Claire sat in chairs.

"That's not fair!" Martin said.
"It's so boring there!"

Dad replied, "First we'll go to the
museum and then to Bear Park."

"We can visit the museum. But I hope there is time to spare. I want to fly my chopper," Martin explained.

"That's fair," said Claire.

"Look at the banner!" Martin cried. "I will see lots of things that fly!"

"This is a rare treat," Dad said. "Claire likes museums. You like things that fly. Let's go inside."

Dad, Martin, and Claire compared the birds there. Martin shared that both birds and choppers fly.

They stared at the birds for a long time. Then they moved on.

"I see rare planes men used long ago!" cried Martin.

"Long ago, some people felt that airplanes were scary," Claire said.

"This was the best!" Martin said. "The museum was not boring. I got to see lots of things that fly. And I got a plane that I can wear!"

Volume 6

Decodable Words

Target Phonics Elements: /ûr/ er, ir, ur

alerted, bird, chirp, dinner, dirt, ever, ferns, first, girl,
Herb, hurt, jerk, lurched, matter, perched, perfect,
perhaps, returned, slower, tender, turned

High-Frequency Words

Review: around, could, looked, out, some, to,
wanted, was

Story Words

friends, hurry, turtle

Decodable Words

Target Phonics Element: /är/ ar

alarm, alarm, car, Carla, charming, dark, far, hard,
Marge, Mark, Marvin, parts, partners, postcard, sharp,
smartest, star, start

High-Frequency Words

Review: how, into, said, to, was, you, your

Story Words

horses, howdy

Decodable Words

Target Phonics Elements: /âr/ *are, air, ear, ere*

air, airplane, bear, Claire, chairs, compared, fair, rare, scary, shared, stared, there, wear

High-Frequency Words

Review: *look, of, people, said, some, to, was,would*

Story Words

museum(s)

Decoding skills taught to date:

Phonics: Short *a*; Short *i*; Short *o*; Short *e*, Short *u*; *l*- Blends; *r*- Blends; *s* -Blends; End Blends; Long *a*: *a_e*; Long *i*: *i_e*; Long *o*: *o_e*; Long *u*: *u_e*; Soft *c*, Soft *g* ,-*dge*; Consonant Digraphs: *th, sh, -ng*; Consonant Digraphs: *ch, -tch, wh, ph*; Three-Letter Blends; Long *a*: *ai, ay*; Long *i*: *i, igh, ie, y*; Long *o*: *o, ow, oa, oe*; Long *e*: *e_e, ee, ea, e, ie*; Long *e*: *y, ey*; Long *u*: *u_e, ew, u, ue*; /ûr/: *er, ir, ur, or*; /är/ *ar*; /ôr/*or, oar, ore*; /îr/ *eer, ere, ear*;/âr/ *are, air, ear, ere*

Structural Analysis: Plural Nouns -*s*; Inflectional Ending -*s*; Plural Nouns -*es*; Inflectional ending -*es*; Closed Syllables; Inflectional Ending -*ed*; Inflectional Ending -*ing*; Possessives (singular); Inflectional Endings -*ed*, -*ing* (drop finale e); Inflectional Endings -*ed*, -*ing* (double final consonant); CVCe syllables; Prefixes *re-, un-, dis-*; Suffixes -*ful*, -*less*; Compound Words; Contractions with '*s*, '*re*, '*ll*, '*ve*; Open Syllables; Contractions with *not (isn't, aren't, wasn't, weren't, hasn't, haven't, can't)*; Inflectional Endings and Plurals (change *y* to *i*); Comparative Inflectional Endings -*er*, -*est*; Irregular Plurals; Abbreviations; *r*-Controlled Syllables